Dinosaur Jokes

Joe King

Abdo Kids Junior
is an Imprint of Abdo Kids
abdobooks.com

abdobooks.com

Published by Abdo Kids, a division of ABDO, P.O. Box 398166, Minneapolis, Minnesota 55439.
Copyright © 2024 by Abdo Consulting Group, Inc. International copyrights reserved in all countries.
No part of this book may be reproduced in any form without written permission from the publisher.
Abdo Kids Junior™ is a trademark and logo of Abdo Kids.

Printed in the United States of America, North Mankato, Minnesota.

052023

092023

Photo Credits: Shutterstock

Production Contributors: Teddy Borth, Jennie Forsberg, Grace Hansen

Design Contributors: Candice Keimig, Pakou Moua

Library of Congress Control Number: 2022917599

Publisher's Cataloging-in-Publication Data

Names: King, Joe, author.

Title: Dinosaur jokes / by Joe King

Description: Minneapolis, Minnesota : Abdo Kids, 2024 | Series: Abdo kids jokes | Includes online resources
    and index.

Identifiers: ISBN 9781098266059 (lib. bdg.) | ISBN 9781098266752 (ebook) | ISBN 9781098267100
    (Read-to-me ebook)

Subjects: LCSH: Jokes--Juvenile literature. | Wit and humor--Juvenile literature. | Dinosaurs--Juvenile
    literature. | Humor--Juvenile literature.

Classification: DDC 818.6--dc23

Table of Contents

Dinosaur Jokes

What do you get if you cross
a dinosaur with a pig?

Jurassic Pork!

Why couldn't the
Apatosaurus stop sneezing?

Because he was Jura-sick!

What do you call a dinosaur with a big vocabulary?
A thesaurus!
OH!
WORDS!
5

Why do Brontosaurus
have long necks?

Their feet smell!

Do you know how long
dinosaurs lived?

The same as short ones.

6

> What's the worst thing that can happen to a Diplodocus?
>
> *A sore throat.*

What do you call a
boring dinosaur?

A dino-snore!

What did the dinosaur
call her T-shirt store?

Try Sara's Tops!

8

Who makes the best prehistoric reptile clothes?
A dino-sewer.
SEW GOOD!
THANKS!
9

What do you get when a dinosaur walks through a strawberry patch? *Strawberry jam.*

What do you get when you cross a dinosaur with fireworks?

DINOMITE!

HEE! HEE!
What happened after the dinosaur took the school bus home.
He had to bring it back.
I thought that banana tasted funny...

What do you call twin dinosaurs?

A Pair o' dactyls!

What do you call a short spiky dinosaur that's fallen down the stairs?

Ankle-is-sore-us.

Ha!
How did the Archaeopteryx catch the worm?
It was an early bird!
I woke up about 150 million years ago!
13

What do you call a
dinosaur car accident?

A Tyrannosaurus wreck!

What do you call a group
of dinosaurs who sing?

A Tyranno-chorus.

14

What do you call a baby T-Rex?
A Wee-Rex!
lowercase t-rex
15

What is a paleontologist's favorite tool?

A dino-saw.

What do you call a gassy dinosaur?

Exstinkt!

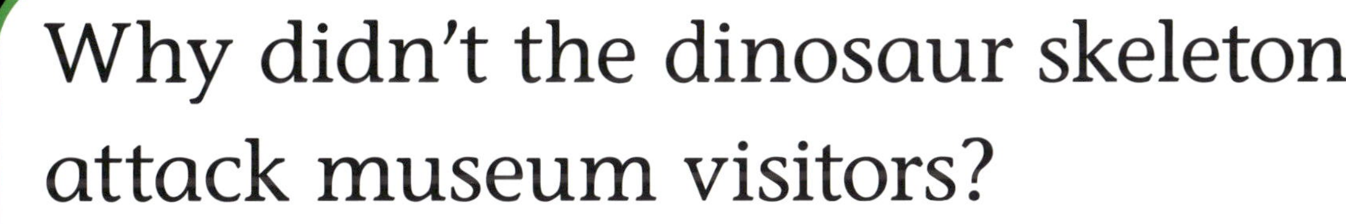

Why didn't the dinosaur skeleton attack museum visitors?
Because it had no guts!

IS it chilly in here?

17

What game does a Brontosaurus like to play?

Squash.

Why was the Stegosaurus such a good volleyball player?

It could really spike the ball!

18

What do you get when a dinosaur scores a touchdown?
A dino-score!
Stay close! My arms don't throw that far!

What do you call a

Spinosaurus that hates losing?

A saur loser!

Which is the scariest

dinosaur?

A Terror-dactyl.

Do you think anything could tricera-top a dinosaur pun?
I dino what to tell you, but probably not.
Top that joke!

21

Joke-Telling Tips!

• Know your audience

• Timing is everything

• Confidence is key

• Go out on a high note!

22

Glossary

paleontologist

a scientist who studies animal or plant fossils for information about life in the past.

pun

a joke using a word that sounds like a different word or has another meaning. Examples from this book are "Jura-sick" (Jurassic) and "Try Sara's Tops" (Triceratops).

Index

Abdo Kids ONLINE

FREE! ONLINE MULTIMEDIA RESOURCES

Visit **abdokids.com** to access crafts, games, videos, and more!